THE MOUSE'S TALE

NICK BUTTERWORTH & MICK INKPEN

D0246167

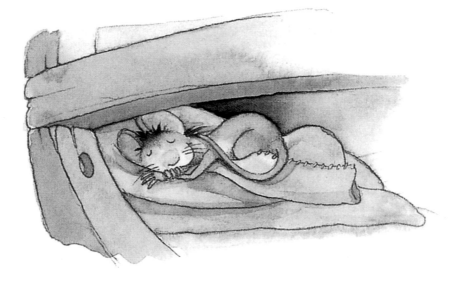

Text and illustrations copyright © 1988 Nick Butterworth and Mick Inkpen
This edition copyright © 2015 Lion Hudson

The right of Nick Butterworth and Mick Inkpen to be identified as the authors and
illustrators of this work has been asserted by them in accordance with the Copyright,
Designs and Patents Act 1988.

This story first published by Candle Books in 2006
in *Animal Tales*. USA edition published
by Zonderkidz ®.

All rights reserved. No part of this publication may be reproduced or transmitted in
any form or by any means, electronic or mechanical, including photocopy, recording,
or any information storage and retrieval system, without permission in writing from
the publisher.

Published by Candle Books
an imprint of
Lion Hudson plc
Wilkinson House, Jordan Hill Road,
Oxford OX2 8DR, England
www.lionhudson.com/candle

ISBN 978 1 78128 175 8

First edition 2015

A catalogue record for this book is available from the British Library

Printed and bound in China, November 2014, LH06

THE MOUSE'S TALE

JESUS AND THE STORM

NICK BUTTERWORTH & MICK INKPEN

CANDLE
BOOKS

Hello, I'm a mouse, a ship's mouse.
And this is my house. It's a fishing boat.

In the evening, when the fishermen
have gone home, that's when I wake up.
I come out and sniff and nibble the
fishing nets.

Well, the other evening, a strange
thing happened.

I'm nosing about on deck as usual
when suddenly, there's a noise. Quick
as a flash I hide behind some old ropes.

Listen, there are footsteps! The
fishermen have come back. Twitch
my whiskers and sniff the air. There's
someone with them.

I can hear the fishermen untying
the boat. Splish splash. I can feel them
pushing it out into the waves. The wind
catches the sail, the mast creaks, the boat
rocks gently and we're heading out to sea.

'It's been a long day,' says a voice I
don't know. 'I think I'll get some sleep.'

Where are we going? We're not going fishing. It's too late for fishing. Where are we going?

We're taking the man with the voice I don't know for a ride in our boat.

The man sits down right next to me and leans his head on my ropes. His hair smells warm. He's not a fisherman.

Everything is quiet except for the waves slapping under the boat.

Soon the man is asleep. I want a better look at him. I creep out from under the ropes. All clear.

The man looks very tired. He has a kind face and he snores.

His breath tickles my whiskers. He can ride in our boat if he likes. I wonder what his name is.

All of a sudden – Flash! Bang! I'm off and running.

Flash! Bang! Lightning and thunder! I scamper up the deck and down my hole.

Flash! Bang! We're in for a rough ride. These summer storms can be nasty.

Now the great black clouds close in.
The sky grows dark.

Big drops of rain begin to splatter on
the deck. The sail flaps and bangs and
gulps the wind.

The storm whips spray across the deck
and giant waves slam the boat.

The boat begins to roll and slide.

One moment up, next moment down. Up and down, up and down with water crashing on the deck and pouring on my head.

And all the while – Flash! Bang! Lightning and thunder. And all the while – Slap! Crack! The wind tatters our sail. And all the while the man sleeps on… and snores.

'Wake up! Wake up! We're going to sink! Wake up! Wake up! We'll all be drowned! Wake up! Wake up! We're going down! Jesus, wake up!'

So that's his name.

Slowly, the man opens his eyes. He blinks and rubs his face and looks around.

And holding on the mast, he stands up straight.

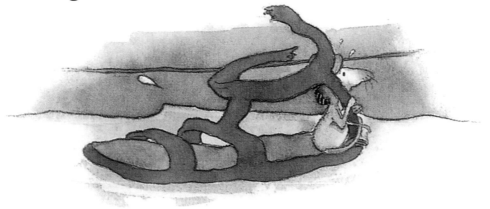

Then stretching out his hand he shouts into the wind.

His voice is firm and strong and very, very loud.

'Peace!' he shouts. 'Be still!'

And straight away the storm does what he tells it to!

The wind dies down, the thunder stops, the sea is calm and all is still.

Can you believe it? The wind, the lightning, thunder, waves and rain all stop! What kind of man is that?

The setting sun peeps out behind a cloud. The men get out the oars to row us home. I shake the water from my paws and ears and settle down to sleep.

So pull the oars, we'll soon be home to tell the tale.

And that man Jesus, if he wants to, he can sail with us again.